MW00678730

Cotton Tales

CottonTales

Life on the Edge of a Cotton Patch

M. Lynn Reddick

with Greg Reddick

Illustrations by Greg Reddick

For book orders, call 1-888-OPEN-1-2-3

Published by Portal Publishing Company
in association with Open Church Ministries

ISBN: 0-9743297-3-8

First Edition, August 2005
10 9 8 7 6 5 4 3 2 1

Printed in Canada

In memory of Dad
—Garnett Gibson Reddick—
who will rise again

INTRODUCTION

IN 1943, WHEN GENERAL GEORGE PATTON, JR. was preparing for the invasion of Sicily in his Italian campaign, Garnett and Annie Laura Reddick were preparing for another kind of invasion in their Southeast Georgia home: a baby boy named Lynn.

Growing up in this rural home with a strong work ethic left little time for trivial pursuits. These were the days prior to the invention of television, plastics, computers, central heat and air conditioning, and—in our house—the telephone. Dad was not a particularly religious man but he did believe in the supernatural: "Idle minds and hands are the devil's workshop," he'd often say.

Summer days found us plowing mules, sawing and splitting wood for winter heat, hoeing the garden where we grew most of our food, and hauling water from the nearby ice house to fill the dry well in our back yard. (You'll hear more about this well in "Fire in the Hole!")

You'd think rainy days would bring some reprieve from all the work. Oh, no. Not with corn to shuck and shell, buckets of bent nails to straighten, and dry peas to sort out for planting in the spring.

In the midst of hard work we had times of relaxation, especially bathing in a Number 3 washtub in the sunny backyard. When my brothers and I outgrew the tub, we'd put a bar of Ivory Soap in our back pocket and head for the pond. Thank goodness for soap that floats!

On our Saturday afternoon trips to town, we learned to stretch the enjoyment of an R.C. Cola and a Moon Pie over most of the afternoon. Such extravagance was financed by picking cotton for a penny a pound (we'd stand on the edge of the cotton patch and wait for daylight) or selling boiled peanuts for a nickel a bag. Picture a barefoot 12 year-old, wearing a straw hat and overalls, yelling at the top of his voice, "Fresh, hot boiled peanuts! How 'bout em?" Talk about an entrepreneur!

Saturday night entertainment came to our house by way of WSM Radio and the Grand Ole Opry. Don't think for one moment that we did not add high culture to our lives with some opry!

My main source of entertainment, however, came from my Granny and Pa, who helped raise us boys. As soon as the work day was done, I'd sail over the fence and through the woods, following the well-worn path to their farmhouse. There on the back porch overlooking the cotton patch, Pa and Granny would tell me stories that stirred my interests and stimulated my imagination.

Now, all these years later, my wife and I live in that house and sit on that back porch. Frequently, our five-year-old grandson, Ethan, finds me rocking on the porch, climbs up in my lap and says, "Papa, tell me that story about you and Nana again." As I begin, the other two grandchildren, Kayla and Sarah, usually gather to listen.

An ancient Proverb claims that "A happy heart is good medicine." And no wonder. The connection between laugher and good health is well established. Even a mere chuckle goes a long way toward releasing stress.

These "Cotton Tales" are life experiences birthed in the warp and woof of daily living. Some of these stories first appeared in the international publication, *The Cotton Patch Papers* over the past several years.

Now, it's time to share some of these stories with you. Perhaps they will stir hope and laughter in your house.

M. Lynn Reddick
on the back porch, 2005

CONTENTS

14

THE PEA PATCH BLUES

or,
How I Learned a Painful Lesson Concerning the
Merit of Shunning Laziness in Favor of Honesty
and Hard Work

IT WAS THE SPRING OF MY EIGHTH YEAR AND time to sow the seeds of harvest, which in this particular case meant numerous five gallon buckets full of peas—itty-bitty peas called *Lady Fingers*. Dad gave my older brother, Lamar, and me the planting instructions, simple enough, and off to the field we went, dragging our buckets through the sand.

After several hours planting pea after pea after pea, I noticed we still had two five gallon buckets left. I scooped up another load in the belly of my shirt and began making my way slowly down the row. After a while my mind started to wander.

"Lamar," I called out. He seemed to be laying them in faster than me.

"What?"

"'Bout time to go swimming, ain't it?"

He didn't say anything, just kept laying them in, peas after pea.

"C'mon," I said. "I'll race you to the pond."

He looked over his shoulder at me. He was thinking about it. I could tell.

He said, "If we go for a dip, it'll be hard to come back up here to work."

"Who said anything about coming back?" I said, and bolted up to grab the bucket handle. I dragged my remaining peas to the end of the row, bent down and started to dig, flinging sand with a fury back between my legs, about like a dog would.

Then, with about four gallons buried, I smiled with pride at the hump in the ground.

I looked up just in time to see Lamar whipping the contents of his bucket across the brush pile at the edge of the woods.

* * *

That night, lying in bed, listening to the rain, I couldn't help but grin at all the fun I'd had that afternoon, whooping it up in the pond. Yessir, I was pretty smart for an eight-year-old, even had a handful of possible explanations ready for the coming day (soon) when the mystery of the non-sprouting peas would present itself.

* * *

About a week or so later, I walked home from school and into the kitchen to find a note on the chopping block with my name scratched on it:

LYNN—
COME TO THE PEA PATCH

I realized it was time to help Dad solve the pea-mystery. And I was ready.

Approaching the pea patch I saw him riding the one-row tractor. I walked closer and saw the peas were sprouting, nice and green and tall.

—and like an explosion it caught my eye, down at the end of the row, the biggest outcropping of a pea-bush anybody ever saw. It was horrible, terrible. My stomach twisted.

Watching Dad, I knew that he knew that I was there, though he never turned to look at me.

I watched him steer that tractor up and down those rows, back and forth, getting closer and closer to where I stood. He had my number, and there was no getting around it.

Rather than go into the details of what happened next, let me just say this: I learned my lesson well!

FIRE IN THE HOLE!

IN 1952 MY FAMILY MOVED TO THE FARM JUST outside of Portal, Georgia, and as soon as Dad finished building the house, he instructed us boys in the fine art of well digging. Armed with pick and shovel, we enthusiastically attacked the X scratched in the sand, a few feet from the back of the house.

After digging a while and toting dirt away in buckets, we soon had to bury two posts to support a crossbeam for the pulley. A rope and bucket made excavation easier, and for weeks my brother and I made that pulley sing.

Then one day, about thirty feet down, we hit

bedrock. I was in the process of lowering the bucket when a sharp sound rose up out of the hole. Three or four more shovel clanks followed, then all was quiet. I turned to call out for Dad but he was already right behind me, approaching with a sour look. He pushed up the brim of his hat and peered into the hole. Two more clanks came up. Dad scratched his head and spat, and let out a long sigh.

* * *

Soon thereafter Dad's cousin Cecil came visiting. As improbable as it may sound, Cecil was actually General George Patton's demolition expert in World War II, and, naturally, Cecil had the perfect solution to our well-digging woes.

"All we got to do is drop fire in the hole to light the fuses and run for cover," Cecil said after taking a swig of his Jack Daniel's and returning the bottle to his back pocket. So we took down the rope, bucket and pulley, and removed ourselves from the immediate vicinity as Cecil, the demolition expert, did his thing.

The thunderous blast bucked the ground and

knocked me back on my sitter, and for a few moments it was like being in a dream. I watched the wooden crossbeam way up in the sky, floating off in a slow spin. Then it began to fall, straightway, coming down like an arrow-shot.

My ears were ringing horribly, and I squinted through the settling dust, watching Dad make a quick damage assessment that went something like this:

The house sagged on one end of the foundation.
Window panes were missing.
Several doors in the house were off their hinges.
Mother's wall hangings now decorated the floor.
Our rock-bottom hole was still a rock-bottom hole.

Mother wasn't home at the time, but she returned shortly thereafter to make her own assessment of the situation, which probably is better left untold.

OH, THE SWEET HERE-AFTER

DURING MY MERCER UNIVERSITY DAYS, I SPOKE at week long meetings in churches, often as many as twelve to fifteen each summer. One meeting in particular really stands out in my mind. My roommate, who was a student pastor, asked me to conduct meetings for six days and nights at his church.

First off, he introduced me to his pianist, a sweet little thing right out of high school. I was so struck by her beauty, I purposed in my heart to add her to the long list of girls I had kissed.

Night after night during the meetings, I carefully

laid my plans. Finally, the week ended. So did my silence. I asked her for a date. She seemed pleased. I was thrilled.

To kiss her on the first date should be no problem, I thought.

It was.

Not only did I not kiss her on the first date, I didn't kiss her on the second, the third, the fourth, the fifth, the sixth, the seventh or the eighth. Who was counting? I was!

Perhaps this church pianist doesn't know how to kiss, I wondered. Maybe she has no interest in kissing! Whatever the reason, I was getting tired of puckering up, making my pass, missing and kissing whatever was near after she ducked. If I'm exaggerating here to illustrate my point I can assure you it isn't by much.

On the ninth date, I complained to her pastor (my roommate).

"I'm going to give that church pianist one more opportunity to kiss me. If it doesn't happen tonight, that's it!"

I drove the usual hour and a half from the

Mercer University campus to her house.

It seemed the perfect evening was at hand. The full moon, the stirring breeze, and the whippoorwill call helped set the romantic stage.

Meandering around on the country dirt roads soon led us to park the '55 Ford at the most sanctimonious place I knew—the backyard of her church. Even the name implied success in my venture. It was the Harmony Baptist Church.

Soon, however, several attempts to convey my growing love and devotion to this church pianist with a kiss utterly failed. She simply wasn't in harmony with my plans.

In desperation I steered the conversation to religion.

"Do you believe in the hereafter?" I asked.

"Why, I most certainly do."

"That's good," I said. "Because if you're not here after what I'm here after, you'll be here after I'm gone!"

As it turned out, I finally *did* kiss that young pianist. Fact is, I married her!

THE CASE OF THE MISSING DIAMONDS

A THIEF BROKE INTO MY HOUSE. IT HAPPENED thirty years ago on a cold Sunday night in December while my family and I were returning from church.

I was in the process of easing the family station wagon into the garage when I noticed the side door was ajar.

A moment like that, when it first hits you, is hard to describe. To see such a sight, sitting in your old familiar car with the love of your life at your side, your kids half asleep in the back, all of you coming home to your warm Haven of Comfort and Security, and then seeing your kitchen door wrenched open—

Reason, let me say, flew the coup. It must have, because I suddenly found myself charging through my house full-tilt, wielding a snow globe that was suddenly—*there*.

Yes, moments like that are hard to translate. Fortunately for him and probably for me, the rascal had already left (although barely; within the hour the police would catch him hiding in the woods behind our house.)

Reason revisited while I was standing on my front lawn among an assembly of curious neighbors and probing police, the latter of whom attempted to procure from my wife and me an inventory of stolen goods:

"So that's it, then?" the officer said finally. "That covers everything?"

"That's about it," I said.

"No!" Linda said, "My diamond earrings. Don't forget my diamond earrings!"

Oh no, I thought, please not the diamond earrings—that gift from a few years back, from me to her, a seemingly extraordinary feat of love during an unusually lean year.

"Can you estimate their value?" the officer said.

A hush fell over the curious onlookers.

"Dr. Reddick?" the officer repeated, "can you approximate the value of the missing diamonds?"

I cleared my throat. "About seven-ninety-five," I muttered, rubbing at my neck.

He scribbled it down, calling out the numbers: "Seven hundred, ninety-five dollars—"

I held out my hand, stopping him. I looked to Linda.

"Honey? About those diamonds...."

After a pause the officer scratched out the numbers and started again. "Seven dollars," he said, "and ninety-five cents." He looked up at me and arched his eyebrow. "Is that correct, sir?"

I glanced back at Linda....

A moment such as that—standing there with those onlookers and an unremitting mental image of the grinning, plaid-suited salesman exclaiming: *They're called cubic zirconias!*—is perhaps even harder to convey.

But it's nothing compared to the explaining I had to do later that night when Linda finally got me alone.

WHOOP-DE-DOO

SKIING DOWN A MOUNTAIN AT BREAKNECK
speed is such an unbelievably exhilarating experience. I couldn't help smiling with anticipation as I
cinched down the straps holding my Atomic Arc
snow skis on top of my new '78 MG BGT. A prom-
ising North Carolina snow was in the air, and it was
finally time to spend a day carving graceful arcs and
winding curves into the side of Sugar Mountain.

As I pulled out of Morganton onto Highway 181
heading north, my mind wandered back to earlier
times, in fact the first two times I took Linda to the

powdery slopes.

We met our friends Ray and Brenda Pridgen there. Brenda was determined to join Linda in this new adventure as they gathered in Base Lodge to dress for the slopes (actually the rope tow area next to the beginner slope called "Easy Street"). It's quite a feat to suit-up for such an adventure: special pants, jacket, rigid boots, poles, goggles, and proper skis.

Linda and Brenda found themselves seated beside a handsome young man who looked as if he just stepped off the front page of *SKI Magazine*. Brenda turned to him with a barrage of questions: *Do we have our ski boots strapped on right? Should we wear our goggles or put them on top of our forehead when we get on the chair lift? How do we hold our ski poles when we push out of the chair lift?*

The young man was hesitant to reply, apparently guarding his secrets.

"Oh, we have one last question," Brenda said, glancing over at Linda. "How do we get up off this bench with these stiff boots on?"

The young man blushed a bit and confided, "Lady, I can't get up off the bench either!"

Linda's second excursion to Sugar Mountain meant graduation: she had done so well mastering the shorter skis on her first trip that I decided to move her all the way up to the real thing, a professional set. Yep, Blizzard Touring Cross Country 210 cm. skis had her name on them.

Also, Linda had graced the gentle slope of "Easy Street" so well on her first day, why not take her to the top where advanced skiers gather, the blustery summit of "Whoop-de-doo"?

As Linda and I pushed past "Easy Street" filled with beginners, the vast 115 acre ski wonderland filled our eyes. I remembered the adage my old mountaineer buddy, Wayne Hawkum, used to say. He had an uncanny way of squeezing one-of-a-kind experiences out of life. He'd spit his Bull of the Woods tobacco, wipe his mouth with his shirt sleeve and say, "Son, if ya want exciting things to happen to yerself, put yerself in places where they can."

"Linda," I said, "Let's go for it. Let's do 'Whoop-ded-oo'!" Ole Wayne will be mighty proud, I thought.

Halfway up it occurred to me that Linda never had been so high on the mountain, ridden a lift so fast, or dropped out onto the steepest ski slope in the southeastern United States. I wanted to make sure she was ready: *Are your goggles tight over your eyes? Are your pole straps securely around your hands? Are you sitting on the front part of your seat ready to push off?*

I looked over and saw that her eyes were the size of saucers. Her face was rigid and expressionless, so apparently focused and determined she was on executing a perfect lift-off. Then our chair passed the top of the exit ramp.

We pushed out of the lift, unaware that one of Linda's ski poles was stuck between my boots.

I sailed out of the chair head first, down the long ramp like someone catapulted from a slingshot. Linda lost her balance and was close behind sprawled out on all fours, yelling at the top of her voice. If that wasn't enough, the swift chair lift dumped about a dozen other skiers down the steep ramp, helping us created such a massive pile-up of arms, legs, skis, and poles that the entire chair lift operation had to be shut down until everyone and everything was untangled.

To this day, I still don't remember how we got down that slope. But I do remember: "Son, if ya want exciting things to happen to yerself, put yerself in places where they can!"

ADVERSITY AND THE ANNIVERSARY

THE DAY BEFORE LINDA AND I WERE TO CELE-brate our tenth wedding anniversary, I was in a fix. It can be tricky sometimes deciding on a gesture suitable to convey the love in your heart to your other half, but being as broke as I was at the time made it even trickier. Compounding my dilemma (unintentionally, of course) was a man named Price, a wheeler-dealer businessman I counted as a close friend. Since he was known to have a certain cre-ative flair (even if at times he seemed a little extravagant), I decided to invite him out to lunch in an effort to pick his brain, maybe get some ideas toward making a silk purse anniversary out of my sow's ear bank account. We were seated at a concrete table on the patio of the local Tastee Freez. It was, after all, my treat.

"By the way," I said. "Tomorrow is the tenth anniversary for Linda and me."

"Congratulations!" he said, flicking a bread crumb off the sleeve of his sports jacket. "I'll bet you have big plans for that special lady."

"Oh, yes," I said. I bit into my corndog and grunted to show I couldn't elaborate on it at the moment with my mouth full.

"Ten years," he said. "Yep, that's a big one. Gotta do it up right, you know, make a lasting impression."

I nodded.

Price paused, waiting to see if I was going to offer up any details.

I kept nodding, and chewing, slowly.

"I sure remember my tenth," he said, and began

chuckling to himself.

I swallowed the corndog quick-like and took my cue.

"Really? What did you do?"

He was about to respond when the loudspeaker barked: *Number 347, your order is ready.* There was a squeal of feedback and then the speaker clicked off. Price stuck his finger in his ear and shook it.

"Good heavens, that was loud," he said. "But yes, we had a blast." He picked up his double cheese-burger and started to take a bite.

I repeated the question: "So what'd you do?"

He chomped down on the burger and the question hung in the air. For a moment I watched the traffic whizzing by just a few feet away.

Then Price took a pull on his straw, swallowed, and said, "Well, first I had a limousine pick us up at the house. I made sure Martha answered the door, of course. Boy was she surprised. Then she got to see the bouquet I had waiting in the car. I thought she'd melt right there in the driveway. We went over to Asheville where I'd made dinner reservations at

Horizons—fanciest restaurant in town, had the chandelier and everything. Five star all the way. After that we checked into the Grove Park Inn, where I'd reserved a honeymoon suite." Here he began chuckling to himself again, remembering it all.

He waved it off with his hand, saying, "Anyway, we had a real good time that night, let me tell you. I know Martha won't *ever* forget that night."

I took my last bite out of the corndog. A bad feeling was creeping up.

But then it hit me, a brainstorm. Suddenly I knew exactly what to do.

* * *

On the big day Linda and I were seated together at dinner. I still couldn't believe such a fancy atmosphere was possible on such a limited budget. All the elements for a romantic evening were in place: the sparkling candelabra, the white linen tablecloth, the flickering candle flame (yes, we were *a la carte*, as the French say), the setting sun over the Blue Ridge Mountains....

I held up my champagne glass for a toast.

"Linda, if King Solomon had met you, he wouldn't have wanted so many wives!"

Linda looked up and met my eyes for the first time. She squeezed my hand a little and her lips parted, but she was interrupted before she could speak—

—*Number 737, your order is ready.*

We winced at the piercing volume, and waited for the feedback to end. When it did, Linda touched the candelabra and said, "This old thing cleaned up well, didn't it?" Then she looked at me and smiled. "You know, you clean up pretty good yourself."

I reached over and gave her a kiss. Then I poured more Pepsi into her champagne glass.

Just then a passing motorist went by faster than he should have and the flame guttered and sputtered in the wake and almost went out. I held up my hand to shield it and waited for the wind-rush to subside.

After we finished our corndogs I sprung for dessert, two soft serve vanilla ice cream cones. They were delicious. Afterward, we loaded the candelabra, linen, glasses and silverware into the trunk of the car. We drove home.

As it turned out, we had a real good time that night. Although it might possibly have been more sow's ear than silk purse (and I'm sure we were quite a spectacle to those patio patrons at the Tastee Freez), I knew that, when I looked at the bottom line, we had shared an evening together that neither of us would ever forget. We had made the most of what we had, and, for us, that was good enough.

THE MAN WHO WASN'T THERE

IF YOU'RE FROM A BIG CITY AND HAPPEN TO FIND yourself some day passing through a small rural town like the one I call home, you might be surprised to find fellow motorists tossing up a finger or two at you as they pass. Depending on how big the city is you're coming from, you might be surprised to find it's not the finger you're accustomed to seeing. That's one of those nice things about being out in rural America; you're surrounded by good, hardworking folk who aren't too busy or preoccupied to nod or wave, even to a passing stranger.

I grew up around Portal, Georgia, and I know many of the people here. But I went off to college in 1961 and spent the bulk of my life living in various cities up and down the eastern U.S. (yes, I've seen my share of big-city fingers, too), and now that I've moved back to the homestead after almost forty years, I can appreciate even more the friendly, passing gestures among members of this great community.

However, over the last couple of weeks I've had several encounters with a local man who has refused to return my greetings, all the while looking me dead in the eye. I don't mean to put down city-life or city-folk, but had something like this happened in, say, downtown Atlanta, I wouldn't have thought twice about it. Sometimes being friendly with strangers can open hatches that are better left battened down, so, understandably, people are often guarded.

The local man in question tends a fruit and vegetable stand located in a roadside yard just within the "city" limits. I pass him every time I go into town and again every time I return. At first when I saw him I would simply lift a finger off the steering wheel as I went by, maybe throw in a nod, but he wouldn't acknowledge me, which was okay for a while.

But after a few days I began to make speculations about the fellow. Maybe he's got a cataract. Maybe he's lost in his own little world. Maybe he's going through some sort of crisis, perhaps a medical condition or a family tragedy.

I decided to conduct a test, see if I could get a better reading on his disposition.

So I became more elaborate with my gestures of greeting. Before long I was lowering my window ahead of time, slowing down, and then throwing my hand out as I passed. I'd shout, "Mornin'!"

But he wouldn't stir.

In a situation like that, about all you can do is shake your head and think, *Wow. Unbelievable.*

I think a part of me became, in a sense, intrigued by this guy, this man in a position of public service who seemed to have the personality of a pine tree. He began to enter my thoughts at unexpected times during the day, and any time I got in the pickup truck to go anywhere he'd immediately spring to mind because I knew without a doubt that he'd be there, waiting. He always was—daybreak to dusk—without fail.

Finally, I made up my mind and even told Linda that I was going to get to the heart of this matter, regardless.

That morning on my way into town I saw him there, just like always, and as I passed I honked the horn real good a couple times and threw my arm out the window.

He didn't budge.

I smiled and thought to myself, *Okay, you just gimme a minute. I'll be right back.*

I took care of some business at the office, made a stop at the post office and then climbed back in the truck. I sat there a moment and formulated my next step.

When I pulled back out onto Highway 80, I remember thinking, *Okay boys, it's show time.*

As I came up on the fruit stand I began steering the truck onto the shoulder of the road, taking it nice and easy. The suspense was killing me, but I kept a cool exterior. I brought the truck to a halt on the edge of the yard, right in front of him.

"Mornin'!" I hollered, grinning ear to ear as if to say, *Bet you won't be ignoring me now.*

Incredibly, he just sat there, didn't say a word.

I kept on grinning and gritting my teeth, holding it in, thinking, *I am not believing this guy!*

A moment or so passed and then the whole thing just began to be too unnerving. He was as unflappable as anyone I'd ever seen. I decided to be direct with him. Just get straight to the point:

"Do you have a problem with me, friend?"

Nothing.

Okay, that does it, I thought.

I stepped out of the truck and began making my way up the grassy incline. Halfway to the stand I looked up to meet his eye. And stopped—

All I could do was stand there for a moment, and shake my head.

"Unbelievable," I said.

I glanced around to see if anyone was looking. The coast was clear so I spun back toward the truck and climbed in and headed home.

Linda saw me coming up the dirt lane and greeted me on the front porch.

"How did it go?"

"Well," I said, "I guess you could say he won. I won't be waving at him anymore."

"Why's that?"

"Because..." I hesitated. Then I just said it:

"Because he's a dummy, that's why."

"Lynn Reddick, I am shocked at you! What a terrible thing to say."

But it was true. That man, a product of the modern world, had good reason to have such a vacant look in his eyes, such a blank expression—for he was in fact a mannequin (I found out later he goes by the name of "Elroy"), a true-to-life dummy.

And, after that experience, I didn't feel so good myself.

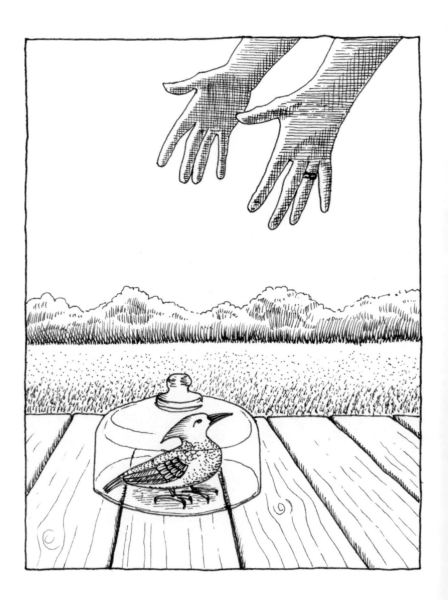

TO KILL A MOCKING-BIRD

(Linda's version)

YESTERDAY LYNN AND I ATE A CLAM CHOWDER lunch, then he headed out to the workshop while I cleaned up the kitchen. I was in the process of raking cracker crumbs over the table edge into my hand when, behind me, something thumped hard against the window.

I jumped—of course the crumbs flew up everywhere—and turned around to see who or what was at my window.

Sometimes during moments of confusion like that all you can do is stand there and watch and wait and listen for clues.

Outside, the bare limbs of the old pecan tree were stirring. But there was no indication.

I walked over to the window and looked out on the porch. And there, lying on its back with its wings stretched out, was a poor little bird. It was colorful, with a speckled breast.

I thought of my two-year-old grandson, who lives a few miles down the road, and how he might like to see such a beautiful bird up close.

So, with a large, glass cake lid, I went out on the porch and placed it over the bird, like a bell jar. First I wanted to show Lynn, but rather than walk out to the workshop, I called him on his cell phone.

"Honey," I said, standing in the kitchen, looking out on the porch, "you must come see this bird. It just flew into the window."

"Did it crack the glass?"

"No, but it's beautiful. You need to come see it

now. It's lying on the porch. "

"Well, dear, I'm a little busy right now. But I'm sure it's a beautiful thing."

Just then the bird started to move. Its wings retracted. It shook its head, and rolled over onto its feet.

"Wait—" I said, "it's alive!"

"That's great, honey."

But the bird flew up against the bowl and was knocked back down. Again it flew against the glass and fell. It started flapping about, flopping and flailing.

"Oh no! It's trying to fly away!"

"Well then, set it free. Why on earth are you holding it captive?"

"I wanted to show it to—" but I couldn't finish for watching the flurry of feathers inside the bowl. "Lynn, quick, I need your help! That poor bird is going to hurt itself!"

"Lift the lid and let it go."

But I couldn't make myself go back out there

near such a horrible commotion.

Lynn must have heard the panic in my hesitation because he said, "Alright, give me a minute."

I set the phone on the countertop and tried not to watch. I felt awful. Then it hit me:

I needed to get out there on that porch and do what needed to be done. I needed to set that bird free. So out there I went, and, wincing, tilted up the lid until the bird flew. It was then that Lynn came trotting around the side of the house.

I called out: "I did it! I did it! I set it free!"

But he didn't seem to hear. His eyes were riveted to the top of the pecan tree. He came forward a few more steps, and stopped.

"Oh, no," he said. "You didn't."

Now I was confused again.

"Quick, go get the shotgun."

"What?"

"Get the gun."

"You can't be serious. My heart just went out on my sleeve for that poor bird, and now you want to shoot it?"

Without taking his eyes off the top of the tree he said, "Linda, that's *the bird*. That's the *woodpecker*!"

Then I knew. For weeks now a persistent wood-pecker has been going to work on our house. It starts early in the morning, usually as Lynn is set-tling down in his study. But before he can slip his shotgun out the side door, it flies off. And it comes back within minutes of Lynn returning to his chair. "That bird," he's said on more than one occasion, "is mocking me!"

So there I was on the horns of a dilemma.

"Linda. Go, get, the gun."

"Alright," I said. "Here I go. I'm going. Would you like a glass of tea while I'm—"

"—*Linda!*"

So off I went, inside, not exactly in a rush, toward the gun rack. I was considering taking him the .22 rifle, as if by mistake, when I heard the back door open and shut.

I met him in the hallway.

"It's gone," he said with a toss of the hand. "It flew away."

I said, "Don't worry, dear. You'll get it."

That was yesterday.

* * *

This morning, early, lying in bed, I heard the familiar *tat-tat-tat* up in the eave of the house. Then, in the next room, I heard Lynn's chair squeak. I listened for a few minutes, waiting, wondering if I'd hear the blast of the gun. I never did, of course.

After a few more minutes, nestled in beneath the quilt, I couldn't help smiling at it all.

Then I got up, and started my day.

THE INCREDIBLE SHRINKING MAN

THE OTHER MORNING AS LINDA AND I WERE enjoying a quiet breakfast, a thunderous crash shook the back end of our farmhouse; we felt it even in the kitchen. With a mouthful of grits, I jumped up from the table and ran down the hall-way to investigate.

The library door, when I tried to open it, met resistance, so I drove my shoulder into it and pushed through, and poked my head into the room. What I saw was not a pretty sight—books were scattered everywhere across the floor, piled up in a great big heap.

Apparently, an upper shelf support in one of the pine bookcases pulled loose and brought down with it all the books and shelves below.

After scratching my head for a moment or two and swallowing the rest of the grits, I realized what I needed: heavy-duty shelf brackets. And since Linda needed to drive into town that afternoon to run errands, I figured I'd let her stop by Lowe's Home Improvement Warehouse, to save myself a trip.

I gave her the instructions, and made sure she understood exactly what kind of brackets I needed. The right brackets were essential if the overloaded shelves were to stay put.

"Got it," she said, walking down the porch steps. "You want the brackets that come in strips about five feet long, that recess into the wood, and that come with adjustable clips."

"That's right," I said. "Only get that kind."

"No problem," she said, and off to tow n she went.

A few hours later she called on the cell phone.

"Lynn, they don't have those shelf brackets here. I've looked and a salesperson has looked. Where else would you like me to go?"

"Linda," I said, "they're there. I've seen them. Let me talk to the salesperson."

A young fellow came on the phone then and I gave a description of the brackets.

"Sir," he said. "We don't carry that kind of shelf bracket."

"Yes you do. I saw them there a few weeks ago. You carry them in two colors, gold and zinc."

"No sir, I'm sorry. We don't have that kind, and, to my knowledge, never have."

Sometimes, when you know something is true, it's frustrating to listen to someone else tell you that it isn't.

"I'd like to speak to another salesperson," I said.

He hesitated.

Then his voice delivered a flat, "Wait a minute."

I waited. Eventually, another salesperson came

on, and again I went through the whole exchange, him saying, *No sir, we don't stock that kind*, and me saying, *Listen to me: yes you do!* and us going back and forth like that for a while. Finally, he said something that stopped me cold.

"Sir, you might ought to try Lowe's."

It hit me broadside, like a shovel. "...This isn't Lowe's?"

"No sir," he said, "This is Wal-Mart."

And with that, all I could think to say was, "Um, could you please put my wife on the phone again, please?"

FACING THE MUSIC

I'M NO STRANGER TO EMBARRASSING SITUATIONS.
I've had my share. Like the time a couple of years
ago when my family and I were heading down I-95,
on our way to Sea World, and I inadvertently took a
wrong exit—into a weigh station for long haul
trucks. I'm sure we were quite a sight to passersby
that afternoon, trapped in our station wagon, sand-
wiched between all those big rigs. When we finally
drove over the scale and it was my turn with the
attendant, he shook his head and said, "Yep, now
I've seen it all."

Was it embarrassing? Sure. Did it sting a little?

Of course, but soon we were riding merrily on our way, everyone laughing (a little too much, it seemed) and me telling stories (to divert attention onto something else, naturally). As it turned out, we had a wonderful vacation.

But as embarrassing as that situation was, it pales in comparison to what I often think of as the Granddaddy of embarrassing moments. This one took place a few years ago during Thanksgiving, also around family; however, this was among a much, much larger gathering.

My father-in-law had stepped up on the den hearth to address me from across the room.

"Lynn, tell me about the piano."

His words chopped off every conversation going. Suddenly every head was turned; all eyes were on me.

The piano in reference was an antique Kimball upright, the same piano that my wife, Linda, learned to play on when she was a child, the piano that, under my father-in-law's hands, filled his grand colonial home with sturdy gospel hymns, daily, year after year... until he decided to pass it down to us, the next generation. We were grateful, elated, and we came to pick it up in my son's new truck. I strapped it down with ropes, secure and tight. Then, not half an hour later, after overtaking a sharp curve in the road (a 90° angle is probably more accurate), my son's truck obtained a small dent behind the cab as a result of the piano shifting, and the piano...well, it came to rest in the ditch on the side of the road, smashed to pieces.

News of the accident would be painful to tell. I knew this, and somehow I managed to put off the telling for three whole months. But the hour soon came, not for my father-in-law to discover the truth, but for me to explain. (He in fact already knew; driving by the accident site one day, he spotted the remains of his long-time companion, realized what had happened, and gathered the shattered pieces to take back home).

I stood there that Thanksgiving day among the familiar crowd with my face glazing and turning an uncomfortable shade of purple, my throat constricting, and the realization growing that all those present were already in the know.

I was fixed in the crosshairs of his stare. Everyone was awaiting my response....

Embarrassing?

Sure.

Did I feel the sting?

You bet.

Did I learn to face all subsequent problems head on?

Absolutely!

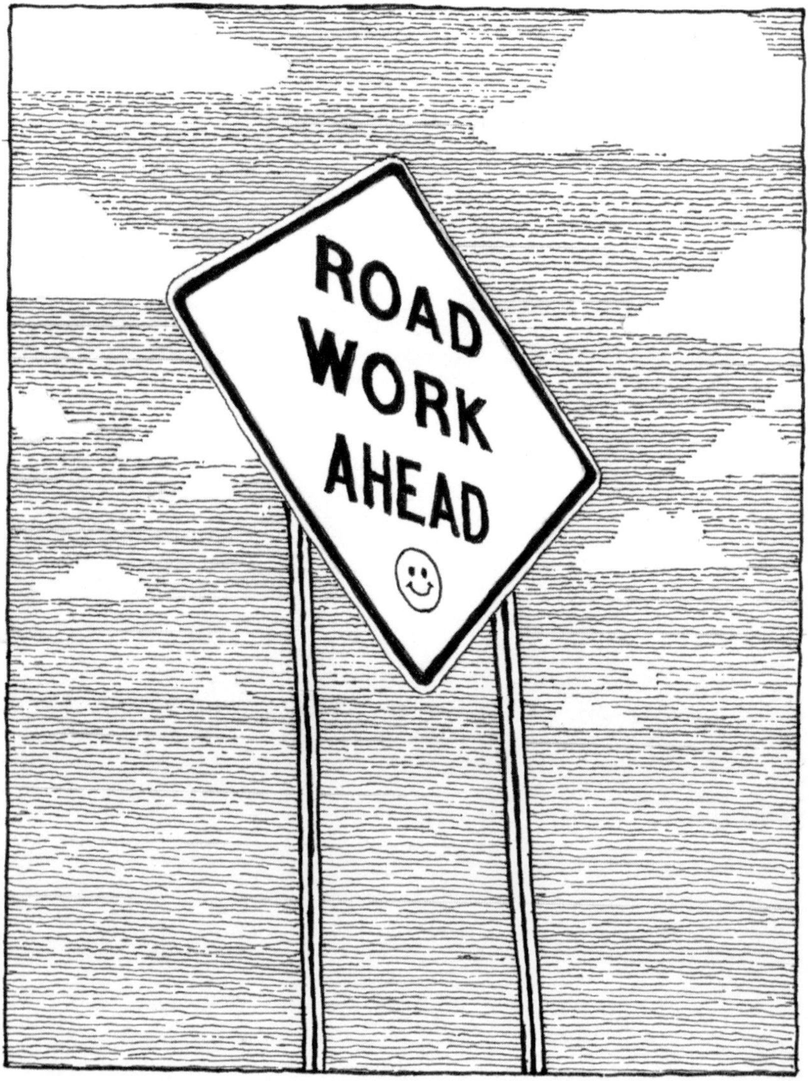
ROAD
WORK
AHEAD

JOHNNY PECULIAR

IT WAS THE MIDDLE OF THE DAY IN THE MIDDLE of July. The air conditioner in my car was wide open. Ahead of me, a road worker was holding a stop sign and waving his arm for me to begin slowing down.

I brought my car to a halt on the newly resurfaced highway, a few feet in front of him.

He broke into a grin, and began nodding his head in approval as a line of vehicles slowly formed behind me. Then he walked over to my window.

I lowered it a few inches and immediately the heat rushed in against my face.

The man took off his hat and held it against his chest and bowed down a little to greet me.

"Good afternoon, sir," he said. "Sure is good to see you today."

From the way he was smiling I gathered that he knew me from somewhere, although to the best of my recollection he didn't look familiar.

"Thank you," I said, somewhat taken aback, not quite sure what to say. "It's good to see you, as well."

"Why thank you, sir. Kind of you to say that. My name is Johnny. I want to apologize for the inconvenience as I know you are an important man with important people to see, but if you'll give me a few moments I'll have you back up to speed in no time."

Listening to him talk I couldn't help but feel impressed with his energy and enthusiasm. His good-natured smile was about the most genuine I'd seen all day.

"Thank you," I said. "I appreciate that."

He returned his hard hat and proceeded back to

the car behind me. I watched in the rearview mirror as he again tipped off his hat and leaned in to greet the driver.

When the pilot truck approached with several vehicles in tow, Johnny came back over to my window.

"Well, here they come," he said, still grinning, "right on schedule."

Johnny waved as each car passed.

Moments later I was driving away behind the pilot truck, and I couldn't help but wonder about Johnny. Was he okay? Yes, it was hot out—maybe the heat had affected his brain. Maybe he was on work release from the nearby mental institution.

Images of the happy road worker stayed with me all afternoon. Then, the next morning on the way into work, he came to mind again.

Before the day was over I ended up driving back over that fresh stretch of highway. And sure enough, he was there, as exuberant as before.

* * *

Johnny didn't suddenly appear in my life a few days ago. In fact, this surprising encounter occurred in 1974—but is as clear today as then.

Why do I still remember his name, his joyful words, and the exact stretch of highway between Drexel and Morganton, North Carolina? Could it be because Johnny was about more than directing traffic or making a buck or two? Could it be that this flagman had something inside that just had to come out and transform the ordinary into something extraordinary. Could it be that one man was determined to be a bastion of good cheer and leave his impression on the lives of passing strangers out there on that scorching hot stretch of asphalt?

Who knows, maybe Johnny was a little coo-coo. But I'm willing to give him the benefit of the doubt.

REMEMBERING DAD
APRIL, 2002

ONE DAY LAST WEEK I CLIMBED IN MY PICKUP truck and headed off down the dirt lane, toward the highway. As I drove I got to thinking about my Dad.

It's funny how certain memories can pop up sometimes without you deliberately reaching for them. Something triggers them, I guess, and there they are, unfolding right in front of you. This particular memory was strong, vivid. As I pulled onto the highway with the window down that cool, bright afternoon, there was a good stretch of country road I was about to lose sight of completely….

"Get on out there, boy!" he shouted. "Tow that line!"

foot wide creek bend. My older brother, Lamar, had the other end of the seining net, and we were wading out deeper. I struggled to keep my footing.

I looked up at Dad on the bank. His eyes squinted back at me from under the brim of his hat. Lamar seemed to be managing his end of the net just fine. Then my foot found a deep spot and my whole shirt got wet real quick. After I caught my breath I hollered out:

"Dad, I can't go out any further. It's too deep."

He shouted back, "Go on. I was seining out there before you were even born. It ain't deep."

I looked down at the water. It was black as pitch. I must have hesitated a bit too long because I heard a splash behind me.

I turned and saw Dad lunging through the water, kicking it up, headed straight at me.

"Give me that," he said, and yanked my end of the net.

Somewhat sheepishly I made my way back over to the creek bank and sat down with my younger bother, Terrell, and turned around just in time to see Dad go under—

He simply disappeared.

There one moment, gone the next.

Dumbfounded, we watched his hat float off down the stream. The only sound was rippling water.

When he came up it was in a sudden gust, arms everywhere, and he began dog-paddling back to the edge.

He stood up out of the water carrying a hard look that dared us boys to even smirk.

"That hole," he said, "wasn't supposed to be there."

The Easter lilies whipping in the wind brought me back. I pressed the button to close the truck window and proceeded on into town.

* * *

At one point in Dad's life he was diagnosed with

terminal cancer and given six months to live.

Three years later, seated on the tailgate of his truck, we talked about the recent test results that indicated his body was completely free of cancer.

A Divine intervention.

"Son, did I ever tell you what happened in the hospital the night after my exploratory surgery?"

"No, I don't believe you did."

"I dreamed Jesus appeared at the foot of my bed. We talked. That night I lost all fear of dying."

These words stunned me, coming from a man who'd never frequented the church house much or talked about Christianity or death—until after this dream.

* * *

About a mile south of town I pulled off the road and drove up the hill to the place where I saw him go under for the second time in my life.

Others were gathered with me that day and they saw it too. Standing there, watching it happen, some may have wondered if he'd be able to rise again.

Not me.

My Dad may have been as intractable and hard-nosed as they come, but I saw a light in his eyes toward the end that I don't think I ever saw before.

Today, exactly fifteen years later, I celebrate the life of a man whose body went under but will rise again on the day an old spiritual song calls "That Great Gettin' Up Morning."

The only thing that stands between a man [or a woman] and what he [or she] wants from life is often merely the will to try it and the faith to believe that it is possible.

—Richard M. DeVos

A Modern Parable

ONCE THERE WAS AN INVENTOR WHO DEVEL-
oped cotton seeds that would yield 25 bales of cotton an acre instead of the normal one or two bales.
He sold the miracle seeds to a young farmer who
followed the inventor's instructions to the letter:
plant the seeds a foot deep rather than the normal
one inch and wait 90 days for them to come up, not
a week or two. "Boll weevils and worms can't hurt
this cotton; even sandspurs won't grow where this is
planted," he said.

When word spread about the farmer planting the

miracle seeds a foot deep, laughter and ridicule erupted over the community. Even family members joined the taunting chorus.

The adventurous farmer held the picture of giant cotton stalks loaded with white bowls firmly in his mind. Day after day he walked over the field looking for cotton sprouts, but found none.

The persistent criticism and mockery, however, did not abate, and soon, weeds of doubt began to sprout in his mind. *Did I really understand that salesman right? Did I bury those seeds for nothing?*

As ridicule increased, so did his doubts. "I must be crazy to believe that story," he confided to his wife, who agreed. "I think I'll plow up the field and plant regular cotton seeds." So he did. On day 89, field hands were busy plowing the field in preparation for replanting.

Meanwhile, at the other end of the county, another farmer was looking across his empty field, chewing his bottom lip, thinking, *Fool or no fool, I'm going to hold on to my dream of that 25 bale an acre cotton patch I see in my head.*

The next morning the farmer walked out on the back porch of his farm house, looked across the cotton field, and grinned. Stretching over the twelve-acre field stood the tallest, whitest cotton stalks he'd ever seen! Not only had the whole field come up over night, but it produced enough cotton bolls, fully opened, to yield at least 25 bales an acre!

A Final Note

The time-path from the back porch of my childhood to today is one of Divine call, testy trial, and human investment.

In 1960, God led me on a 38-year vocational path as pastor in several Evangelical churches. This path widened in 1998 when my wife and I began working through Open Church Ministries and forming the nation's first Bible college that concentrates on open, interactive meetings and small group dynamics, particularly house churches.

"For you, O God, tested us; you refined us like silver." (Psalm 66:10). Singer Ray Charles stated the certainty of trials another way: "There's nothing written in the Bible, Old or New Testament, that says, If you believe in Me, you ain't going to have no troubles." And Charlie Brown believes that "it always looks darkest just before it gets totally black." Trials and troubles in our family indeed turned black in April of 1975 when my wife became the victim of a rare condition that left her entire body numb for seven years. The ensuing emotional trauma drove us on a journey that led to her miraculous healing on April 21, 1982, which changed our lives and ministry profoundly.

Investment of time and energy in other people has been a life-long call and goal. Early on, I had folks around that believed in me, elevated my self-worth, and challenged me to treat every person as "somebody." More than back porch philosophy, this principle was echoed by my best friend, a Carpenter from the Middle East, who taught me (through trial and error) to forgive and bless rather than curse. We put this principle in a potentially life-changing book, *The 2 Minute Miracle*. Read it and you will discover a biblical treasure hidden for centuries, the key to unlocking the storehouse of blessings for you and others.